Creating
Children's
Art Games
for Emotional
Support

of related interest

Creative Expression Activities for Teens
Exploring Identity through Art, Craft and Journaling
Bonnie Thomas
ISBN 978 1 84905 842 1

Creative Coping Skills for Children
Emotional Support through Arts and Crafts Activities
Bonnie Thomas
ISBN 978 1 84310 921 1

Arts Activities for Children and Young People in Need
Helping Children to Develop Mindfulness, Spiritual Awareness and Self-Esteem
Diana Coholic
ISBN 978 1 84905 001 2

Self-Esteem Games for Children
Deborah M. Plummer
Illustrated by Jane Serrurier
ISBN 978 1 84310 424 7

Social Skills Games for Children
Deborah M. Plummer
Illustrated by Jane Serrurier
Foreword by Professor Jannet Wright
ISBN 978 1 84310 617 3

The Expressive Arts Activity Book
A Resource for Professionals
Suzanne Darley and Wende Heath
Foreword by Gene D. Cohen MD PhD
Illustrated by Mark Darley
ISBN 978 1 84310 861 0

Creating
Children's
Art Games
for Emotional
Support

Vicky Barber

Jessica Kingsley *Publishers*
London and Philadelphia

First published in 2011
by Jessica Kingsley Publishers
116 Pentonville Road
London N1 9JB, UK
and
400 Market Street, Suite 400
Philadelphia, PA 19106, USA

www.jkp.com

Library of Congress Cataloging in Publication Data
Barber, Vicky.
  Creating children's art games for emotional support / Vicky Barber.
      p. ; cm.
  ISBN 978-1-84905-163-7 (alk. paper)
  1. Play therapy. 2. Art therapy for children. I. Title.
  [DNLM: 1. Child. 2. Play Therapy--Handbooks. 3. Adolescent. 4. Art Therapy--Handbooks. WS 39]
  RJ505.P6B36 2011
  618.92'891653--dc22
                          2010026403

British Library Cataloguing in Publication Data
A CIP catalogue record for this book is available from the British Library

ISBN 978 1 84905 163 7
eISBN 978 0 85700 409 3

Printed and bound in the United States

To my granddaughter Lucy and my godson Leon,
who are both very special and inspirational.

Also to my children, Victoria and James.
Without them this book would never have
happened – they give meaning to my life.

Acknowledgements

A big thank you to Oliver Daniel-Barnes for the sensitivity and humour conveyed in his illustrations. My thanks too to all the young people who tried and tested the games. To the City University students who gave freely of their time with ideas and criticisms. A special thank you to Maria Galvez for the energy she put into running the games with the young people. Last but not least a big thank you to my dear friend and colleague Eileen Bellot who has always been a tower of strength and an inspiration to me.

Contents

Part II Creating Games for Improving Self-Esteem and Confidence

Part III Creating Games for Raising Self-Awareness

Useful Templates and Resources

Introduction

The ideas for this book came to me many years ago while watching my children's reactions to presents received for birthdays and Christmas. Often the toy would be briefly inspected and then cast aside for the greater delights of the box and wrapping-paper debris – the excitement they had crawling in, out and amid it showed just how much fun could be had out of what we consider to be 'rubbish'. So we (my son, aged four, and I) went on to engage with a host of toy-making activities. The toys we created together gave him huge amounts of enjoyment, especially in the creation stages – he learnt how to sew, cut, paint and paste, and his pride in the end result was immense. Yes, he had hours of fun playing with and disappearing into the toys with his friends, but I couldn't help but remember how much more he got out of the making stages. This is what I tapped into when I decided to write this book – just how powerful and important creating, ownership and empowerment is to a child or young person.

The importance of game-playing as a psychological intervention can be traced back as far as the early 20th century when the Austrian psychoanalyst Melanie Klein (1882–1960) developed her play therapy techniques, in which toys and play were used much as dreams and free association were as part of the analytic process for adults. Following on from Klein, D.W. Winnicott (1896–1971), an

English paediatrician, used games as part of his analysis practice. In his book *Playing and Reality*[1] he summed up his thoughts around the significance of playing:

> If the therapist cannot play, then he is not suitable for the work. If the patient cannot play, then something needs to be done to enable the patient to become able to play...

Winnicott used games to engage and communicate with his patients very successfully. It is from his 'Squiggle' game that the idea of the Scribble games originated. More recently as a practitioner, I found Marian Liebmann's book *Art Therapy for Groups*[2] invaluable, especially in my early days as a newly trained art therapist. She directly inspired and stimulated my thinking and convinced me that there is a very real place for game-playing in the world of art therapy and beyond, in fact for anyone working with children.

The words *play* and *game* immediately instil in us a feeling of lightness and fun – thoughts like 'I don't need to worry about this as it's only a game' or 'It's only a bit of fun' enter our minds and place us on a different plane. Our bodies and minds relax and a frisson of excitement sweeps through us. Similarly, mention the word *game* to children and they're instantly with you, they become a captive audience. Game-playing is as natural to children as eating and sleeping. It's the way they assimilate all the learning that continuously takes place in their daily lives. Playing, exploring, touching, feeling, tasting and smelling are all part of a child's life, so why not use these aspects of life to assist when things go wrong or become confusing?

In my work as an art therapist within schools, Winnicott's words once again echoed in my head, and this is what led me to devise art games that I felt could be used with children to confront their particular problems and issues. Consequently I set out to find strategies to help them explore what is going on and, it is hoped, enable them to come up with solutions.

For instance, working with a group of nine-year-old boys who had problems with anger, socialisation and self-esteem, we first had to

1   Winnicott, D.W. (1971) *Playing and Reality*. London: Routledge, p.54.
2   Liebmann, M. (1986) *Art Therapy for Groups: A Handbook of Themes, Games and Exercises.* London: Routledge.

enable them to talk about situations that drove them to lose control, and then we looked at how they could have acted differently to the way they did. From the role-play they engaged in it became very clear to me that they were greatly influenced by the media, films and computer-animated games. Violence and aggression seemed to be what they aspired to. When even the 'good guys' acted in an untoward way in order to ensure that good conquered evil, it was no wonder these boys thought this was the way forward. It was interesting that when we were sorting out roles no one wanted to play the victim, they all wanted to be the 'bad guy'. If they agreed to play the law enforcer this too was delivered in an aggressive way, as if this was how reality was. They had no problem being shot down and dying; it seemed that this was part of life. I knew I had my work cut out to try and turn things round and let them learn that there was a right way and a wrong way, and that good was more desirable than evil. It was a long, arduous journey, but we had made considerable progress by the end of the sessions. One of the last pieces of work the group engaged in was that of inventing a game that was tailor-made to help them with their particular problems. They invented a town especially for this. Through discussion about their needs and their problems a wonderful town with a difference grew. I asked 'What would you need to help manage your problems?', and one bright individual called out 'Psychology'. We explored what he meant and quite soon the town had areas such as sports, retail therapy, art/music/drama therapy, a space they called 'emotions' and a beach – the presence of which I think would help with a lot of life's problems for many of us, let alone that of the average nine-year-old. I knew that we had found something of value when they wanted to forgo their playtime to extend their sessions with me.

This confirmed thoughts I had been having for some time that if children are given the opportunity and space they are great inventors and fearless creators, brimming with such amazing ideas. It's as if they value their own creations more than manufactured games. This is what makes this book unique and different, as its main focus is on the making of the game, the actual hands-on creation of it. The emphasis is on the empowerment of the children/young people. By enabling them to externalise their own ideas and thoughts, there is no doubt that their confidence will soar.

The games in this book follow this format – time for the game to be thought through, discussed and formulated, which is titled 'Creating the game', and then 'Playing the game'. Although the games sometimes include competitiveness, winning and scoring as elements of game-playing, these are almost an irrelevant part of the process. Being creative, understanding and experiencing through play are what I am primarily aiming for. The areas covered relate to raising awareness of self and then of others, as in so doing the children can gain a better understanding of how their world operates, why things may go wrong and how things can then be worked through, corrected, accepted and developed. In game-playing there is an unspoken rule that there are winners and losers, but this can change by using strategies and making choices. It reminds me of a very old saying someone wrote in my autograph book when I moved away from Sri Lanka, which has always stayed with me: 'When the one great scorer comes to write against your name he marks not that you won or lost but how you played the game.'

Many of these games are reminiscent of games played when we were children but have been altered to meet the criteria. The book had to be fun as I feel humour is important, even in the world of

therapy, so I used 'Lucy and Leon', my granddaughter and godson, to lead the reader through the game-playing. Let's meet Lucy and Leon.

Lucy and Leon are ordinary children who love game playing. Lucy can be demure and ladylike at times, but together with Leon she becomes a more physical adventurer, willing to take chances and becoming a fearless explorer. Leon on the other hand is very much a football-playing, physical go-getter, who does, however, have his quiet moments, especially when read to. So you see they complement each other perfectly. They are ageless as at times they appear young and naive, but at others they appear seasoned beyond their years.

They are portrayed as cartoon characters who are continually grappling with the games they are engaged in, much as cartoon characters do when they are trying and failing to achieve what they want. I chose Lucy and Leon for this as they are such different children from such different backgrounds.

How to Get the Most Out of This Book

Use the games as a starting point. See them as the beginning of something exciting and not merely as games to be copied and played. Each game has the potential to trigger off a great deal of thinking, conversation and ideas that will undoubtedly empower the children taking part.

As with all new things the children will view you as the expert, when really *they* are the source of all new and exciting thinking, as they are focused and are able to live in the moment. You on the other hand have many things like the matters of success, outcomes and results cluttering up your thought processes.

The important part of the game is not the playing of the game but the forming of it. Here the empowerment process starts, with the conversations and drawing out of information, then the actual making of the game and ultimately playing it. The next important part of each game is the feedback and getting the children to give you their ideas inspired by the game they have just played. Don't get defensive if a game hasn't gone as you planned, rather show that you are looking to them to adjust, rewrite and reform the game. Ownership can be empowering, so encourage this whenever possible.

Step-by-Step User Guide

Step 1

Read through the whole book in order to get a sense of the games, what they are about, and how they could help your particular children. Don't be put off by the age criteria; these are intended only as an approximate guide and can be adapted in most cases.

Step 2

Once you have selected a game, familiarise yourself thoroughly with it. Gather all the materials suggested; again this can be changed depending upon what is available. Don't be put off playing the game just because you don't have the 'right' materials; use what you have.

Step 3

The pre-game activity is important. The discussions and suggestions that arise are very much an empowering ownership process. You start off this part, but make sure that the children's input is listened to and acted upon. If it takes longer than suggested, then so be it. Don't hurry things along in order to play the game. Look on playing the game as the icing on the cake and the creating as the cake. Make sure that each child has an envelope/folder where necessary to preserve his or her creation.

Step 4

If your group is small or if you are using this in a one-to-one session, make sure you adjust the rules accordingly, ensuring that each group member has at least one turn. Time-keeping is important in this section. With many of the games it will be useful to ask the group for their suggestions for how the game may be varied.

List of Materials

White paper of varying sizes

White card of varying sizes

Coloured marker pens, both thick and thin

Pencils

Erasers

Rulers

Coloured pencils

A stapler and staples

Masking tape

Clear sticky tape

Glue stick

White glue (PVA)

Paint – black, white, red, blue, yellow

Paint brushes – thick and thin

Scissors

Oil pastels

Fabric for blindfolds

Sand timer

Dictionary/thesaurus

Whiteboard

Flip chart

String

Shoe box

Sticky labels

A book about rabbits

A scoring sheet

Crayons

Coloured counters

Dice

The templates and resources at the end of this book

Note: This is a comprehensive list of things which you will need at some point but obviously not all the time.

Case Studies

Let Rorschach Help Your Story

This exercise (see p.57) brought up very powerful creative writing with some teenagers who were going through troubled times. I was particularly moved by their poems and would like to share these with you to give you a flavour of just how powerful this exercise can be.

This poem was written as a result of the death of a friend. All this young person could see in her image were things relating to this very sad event. Words such as grief, sadness, wings, mixed emotions, angel – she called it 'Always'.

Always

Sadness is what fills my heart
Forever and always
I will remember you
Forever and always
I will try to get over this
Forever and always
But I can't
Because of you

I will remember all the good times
And because of you I have a smile on my face
Because of you everyone is united
Forever and always

This poem was created by a young person who had confidence and self-esteem issues.

The Monster Inside

It scares me
I fear it
I wish it would go away
It comes after me at night
It is my nightmare I fight
I try to fight it but
It keeps coming back
I try to run away
But it catches me
If I let it take control
What might it grow to be
When I look in the mirror
It stares me in the face
It looks sad, lonely and misplaced
I have to shut my eyes before it's too late
It's taken control of me
What have I become?

Scribble Exchange

Working with a group of boys aged eight who had issues to do with self-esteem and anger, playing this particular game (see p.105) highlighted some of their very real anxieties. Through their creative writing it was clear that Denis had self-esteem issues and his story shows just how he would solve things for himself. Denis's images were the number 3, eyes, a hand and a large person, and he wrote the following story.

Once upon a time there was a person with 3 eyes and a big hand and everyone was laughing at him. So one day he went to the hospital, then they took off one eye and then he had two eyes left. Then next he came out of hospital and they said he should go to the gym 'cause of his weight, so nobody would laugh at him again. He was happier after all.

Cube Fun

Tina

Tina, a 13-year-old girl of Asian origin, had experienced art therapy previously and so was quite positive in joining in the sessions. She used her time with us very well and integrated with the other group members. However, on about the third week she was confused about the time of the session and so arrived too early and then didn't come back when she was supposed to; consequently she missed her actual session in which the group were making a cube through which to explore their emotions (see p.71). The following week, on discovering what she had missed, she became very bad tempered and depressed, and although she was offered the opportunity to create her cube she refused to do so. The facilitator suggested that she could externalise her anger on paper, which she readily did; the image that emerged captured her angry mood beautifully. She visibly changed as she vented all her negativity onto the paper; she then said she would like to create her cube as she felt so much better. I felt that this was truly art therapy in action.

Later she talked about the sessions in a video diary: 'It's really good so far…they asked us to open up, I think it's really good that we have this.'

John

A group of young teenagers I worked with found this game particularly vibrant and engaging. When making his cube John had identified that one of his problems was that he couldn't pass a shop without having to spend money buying things he didn't really need. When it came to his turn to talk about this particular problem he genuinely felt quite helpless to come up with a solution. However, the rest of the group became quite animatedly helpful, making excellent suggestions to help him. They suggested things like perhaps having no money on him would help, or taking a route that didn't go past shops; rewarding himself for being strong enough to resist temptation was yet another suggestion. The interaction between the group was admirable, and John felt truly supported and heard.

Shape Town

This game (see p.95) originated when working with a group of primary-aged children in an after-school art club. The children had spontaneously formed themselves into two small groups and each group wanted to form their own town. They were clear about being quite different from each other and after much discussion it was decided that one town would be completely round and the other completely square. The decision they arrived at was that simply everything in the town including people and animals had to be either round or square. The children had great fun, especially when it came to forming the people and animals, and they were very territorial in that their shape simply could not be used by the other group. In the feedback, issues such as the importance of identity and individuality were very visible. It highlighted just how much they valued that sense of belonging.

The school was an Inner London school that had quite a diverse ethnic mix, and I found that this game was therefore quite pertinent.

A Town of Our Own

I have included this as it illustrates beautifully how a wealth of ideas tumble forth from children. With the right environment and encouragement they will engage and show what is important to them and how they perceive the world generally.

Whilst working with a group of young boys aged nine and ten they suggested and went on to form their own town. From this time on the game they chose to play was always the one they had invented themselves, using objects such as figures and cars found in the room to enhance their play. They covered things like personal relationships, sexuality, sport and socialisation in their fantasy play.

In their town designed on card they had included a school, a hotel, a youth club, a newsagent's, a fast-food restaurant, cycle and car parks, flats, a bakery, roads, recycling bins, a playground, litter bins and traffic lights. I felt all of this reflected so well their own everyday environment and what they felt was important.

It was interesting to note that there was a natural leader who the others looked to for ideas and encouragement.

As a result of the last town a group member said that they should make another town, and I suggested perhaps it could be different and help with their problems and issues this time. After a lot of discussion someone came up with the idea of a town to help them deal with their personal problems both in and out of school. They then went on to form a very large, almost room-size town which had a different coloured background for each section, such as Red for Sports, Yellow for Seaside, Green for Retail Therapy and Blue for Psychology (all their own ideas). It was interesting that topics such as yoga and anger management had infiltrated their world of fast-moving action films and games. A border was formed right round, this being the path to be followed by each player. They used their own particular skills in the formation of this town. Adrian had the most ideas about what went into the Psychology section, so this became his responsibility. Nick, the ideas person, helped everyone generally, as well as being responsible for Retail Therapy. Dan looked after the Sports section and Kit the Seaside section. Once the central area was completed they went on to make cards relating to each section with tasks on each card should a person happen to land on particular squares.

This game took a few weeks to form and during this period they were not bored in the least. They then spent quite a bit of time playing the game. On reflection I felt that forming the game and the interaction between them was where the real work and progress lay. Playing the game felt like the icing on the cake – tasty, but not as substantial as the cake.

Part I
Warm-Up Games

Pass the Ball

Objective:	To expand imaginative thinking.
Playing the game:	A ball is passed round to music; when the music stops the person holding the ball is given a colour by the person on their right. Then the person with the ball has to think of three different things in that colour, e.g. a bus, fire engine, post box…

Guess the Colour

Objective:	To use role-play and colour playfully.
Playing the game:	One person goes out of the room. The group selects a specific colour and an object/animal in that colour The person is then invited back and has to guess what the colour is from the clues offered. The clues given should be of the objects, animals, etc. (e.g. elephant, bus, things in that colour).If the person guesses right they choose the next person to go out.

Make the Sound of…

Objective:	To use sounds playfully.
Playing the game:	One person thinks of something and makes its sound (e.g. a car, cat, bird, etc.). The group has to guess what it is. The person who guesses right goes next.

Guess What?

Objective:	To use air drawing to inspire the imagination.
Playing the game:	One person draws an object in the air (e.g. a chair, mirror, etc.) and the group has to guess what it is. The first person to do so correctly goes next.

Feel What It Is…

Objective: To inspire the imagination.

Playing the game: Standing in a circle, the first person draws on their neighbour's back and this is passed round; the last person has to reveal what it is.

Whose Nose Is It?

Objective: To be creative with the minimum of information.

Playing the game: Each person in turn draws a nose belonging to an animal and the person who guesses it correctly goes next. The drawing could take place in the air too.

Getting to Know Each Other

Objective: To learn names.

Playing the game: Each person thinks of a positive/fun way to describe and introduce themselves using the first letter of their name (e.g. Lovable Lucy, Likeable Leon). Then in a circle each person takes turns to present their name with a description using mime (e.g. Lovable Lucy – here she can hug herself and say her name).

Colour Appreciation

Objective: To enable mixing and mingling.

Playing the game: On cue the group is invited to find another person wearing the same colour as themselves (this could go on to hair colour, eye colour, etc.).

Quick Colour Responses

Objective:	To reflect on similarity and differences.
Playing the game:	The facilitator calls out a colour and asks for a quick response to it (e.g. 'red' – blood, cherry, bus). They then get group members to call out the colours.
Variation:	Responses have to be of feelings only (e.g. 'red' – anger, passion, etc.).

Feeling Is the Object

Objective:	To develop powers of feelings.
Playing the game:	Several objects are placed in a bag. The bag is passed round and each person picks an object randomly. They then have to say something about the object – if possible, something to do with a memory.
Variation:	This game can be turned into a truth-and-lie one by making up a story around the object and the group having to guess whether it's the truth or a lie.

Part II
Creating Games for Improving Self-Esteem and Confidence

Pushing the Boundaries

Objectives:	To teach children about the importance of boundaries and in turn to build up confidence.
Age range:	8+
Group size:	3 to 10
Materials:	Paper, coloured marker pens, box
Creating time:	40 minutes
Playing time:	20 minutes
Creating the game:	Explain the aims and rules of the game. Have a discussion about what boundaries are and give examples. Ask each child to write down on a piece of paper a situation that pushes boundaries. Then fold these up and place in a box (make as per instructions on p.125).

Playing the game: One issue is selected from the box for role-play. A boundary holder (BH) and a boundary pusher (BP) are picked. The rest of the group are boundary decision makers (BDM) and they control the movement of the BH and BP. A boundary line is placed in the middle of the room with the BH and BP as far back on either side of the boundary line as they can go. Then the role-play begins. The BP begins stating the problem and takes one step forward; the BH responds, also taking a step forward. The group decides who goes forwards or backwards. If the retort is not good then the BDM may ask the relevant person to move back. The person to reach the boundary line is the winner.

Charades with a Difference

Objective:	To enable the child to confront difficult emotions they may have. Excellent for confidence building.
Age range:	7+
Group size:	3 to 10
Materials:	Card, glue stick, scissors, Emotion Sheets
Creating time:	40 minutes
Playing time:	20 minutes
Creating the game:	Prior to the session the facilitator should have a set of five blank cards cut out (the size of a playing card) for each child as well as photocopies of the 'Emotion Sheets' to hand out (see pp. 133–139). Each child should then choose five emotions which they should keep

secret. They should then cut and stick each selected emotion onto the card, a separate card for each emotion.

Playing the game: Each child, in turn, is then invited to pick a card. Still keeping it secret they will then enact that particular emotion and the rest of the group has to guess what emotion it is. The facilitator should keep score of the right answers; the person who guesses right should then have their turn.

The facilitator should check how the young people felt playing this game and whether there were any emotions that were easier or more difficult to enact. They are invited to suggest how else their 'emotion cards' could be used.

Run Rabbit

Objectives:	To develop strategies for dealing with trauma and when confronted with danger to be able to get out of it.
Age range:	5+
Group size:	6 to 10
Materials:	A large space, a book about rabbits, thin card, string, scissors
Creating time:	40 minutes
Playing time:	20 minutes
Creating the game:	Explain the aims and rules of the game. Read out the main characteristics of rabbits. Discuss what kind of danger is likely to be experienced by the rabbit. Divide half the group into rabbits and half into the dangers.

Get the dangers to make a red band for their heads; the rabbits make ears (use rabbit's ears template on p.129).

Playing the game: The rabbits move around the room running, shaking and dodging around each other and generally enjoying the environment. Meanwhile the danger children huddle in a corner deciding what particular danger they are. Then suddenly the danger appears and the rabbits freeze. The danger announces what they are and selects a victim. If the victim is able to give a good reason why they should not be attacked by the danger they can run off into safety. If they can't they go off to the danger's den.

Variation: Other animals may be used by just changing the ears.

Whatever
(Sticks and Stones)

Objectives:	To teach techniques for brushing off abusive words/actions and to transform negative into positive, leading to a sense of empowerment. To learn appropriate responses to abusive behaviour.
Age range:	7+
Group size:	2 to 10
Materials:	Paper, coloured marker pens, flip chart
Creating time:	40 minutes
Playing time:	20 minutes
Creating the game:	Explain the aims and rules of the game. The discussion produces a list of abusive and bullying words and actions; put this up on a whiteboard or flip chart. Get the group to

screw up a ball of paper for each insult on the list.

Playing the game: The group is divided into two lines (say five in each line). Taking turns the first child throws one of the paper balls at the child opposite.

1. The child responds in the way they normally would to an insult of this kind – catching the ball, dodging it, catching it and throwing it back, etc. When everyone has had their turn, a discussion is started and examples of responses asked for. It's back to the board for brainstorming alternative responses to the insults.

2. When the paper is hurled at the child again, they catch it if they can and use the positive statements from the board. For example, 'What you have just said is hurtful and untrue', 'My feelings get hurt when you say that to me', 'I want you to stop saying those things to me'. Then the paper ball is binned.

What Am I Really Like?

Objective:	To build up confidence in self and others by looking at positive attributes.
Age range:	8+
Group size:	2 to 10
Materials:	Paper, coloured marker pens, scissors, pencils
Creating time:	20 minutes
Playing time:	20 minutes
Creating the game:	On separate small pieces of paper write down the names of all the participants; fold and place them in an open box (use instructions on p.125). Then divide the participants into two groups. Invite each person in both groups to pick one name from the container. Now get each person to draw one particular

unique characteristic of the person they have picked (e.g. a splash of yellow representing a happy, sunny person).

Playing the game: One person is invited from each group, in turn, to show their drawing and talk about the characteristic. Then the other group has to name the person. If they succeed, their group gains a point; if they don't, the drawing group gets the point. Scoring could be kept by the facilitator. The group with the most correct guesses wins.

The group are encouraged to reflect on the game and make suggestions for other games.

Guess What It Is

Objective:	To encourage and expand self-awareness, thereby building up confidence and independent thinking.
Age range:	7+
Group size:	2 to 10
Materials:	White card, coloured marker pens or coloured pencils, sand timer, scoring sheet
Creating time:	20 minutes
Playing time:	20 minutes
Creating the game:	Explain the aims and rules of the game. Suggest the theme of animals, and lead a discussion about the characteristics of animals including movement and sounds.

Playing the game: There are two teams – Team A and Team B.

Each child draws an animal on their card. Each team separately puts their cards into a pack and shuffles it. Then one person from Team A chooses a card from the pack and will mime the animal for Team B, who have to guess what animal it is.

Scoring could be kept by the facilitator – a point for each correct guess.

Variations: The children could be asked to focus on another category rather than animals and then cards could be made and played with in much the same way.

This game may be used in one-to-one sessions – here the facilitator could be the opponent.

Contour Drawings

Objective:	To build up confidence and independence through self-exploration.
Age range:	7+
Group size:	1 to 10
Materials:	Large paper, coloured marker pens or coloured pencils, sand timer
Creating time:	15 minutes
Playing time:	15 minutes
Creating the game:	Working in pairs, Person 1 lies on the paper in whatever position they like, and Person 2 then draws round Person 1.
Playing the game:	Each person fills in their contour shape. A timer can be set for this. Then each individual

has to talk about their image. Points could be given for content, creativity and courage to share.

Variation: Each pair can exchange contour images and fill in their partner's image illustrating the feelings they have about their partner.

Drawing Together

Objective:	To build up sensitivity towards individual members of the group and awareness of allowing equal input.
Age range:	7+
Group size:	5
Materials:	Large paper, coloured marker pens, oil pastels or coloured pencils, sand timer
Creating time:	10 minutes
Playing time:	20 minutes
	If the group is large they can be divided into two groups and the collective time could be 30 minutes.

Creating the game: Explain the aims and rules of the game. Before the image is formed get the children to discuss what the theme is going to be (e.g. a farm, town, seascape, person, etc.). Ensure that each child takes a turn in contributing to the image, with a time limit of, say, one minute per child.

Playing the game: On completion of the image, the whole group has to turn their backs to the image and they are asked relevant questions. For example, if it's a farm, 'How many animals are there?' or 'Where is the farmhouse?'

Variation: Teams could be formed, together with a scoring system.

Drawing with Different Body Parts

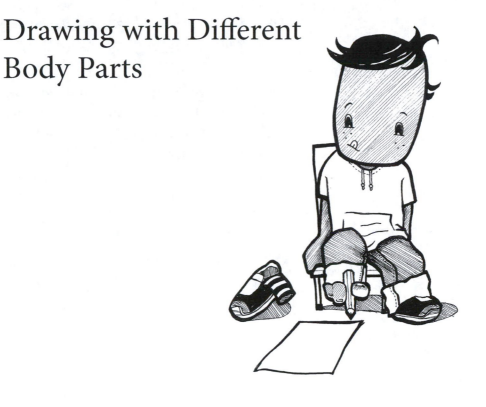

Objectives:	To identify how versatile and adaptable children/young people can be and to raise awareness of how this growth in confidence can happen.
Age range:	7+
Group size:	1 to 10
Materials:	Large paper, coloured marker pens or coloured pencils
Creating time:	20 minutes
Playing time:	15 minutes
Creating the game:	Explain the aims and rules of the game. Divide the group into two teams. Invite one person from each team to draw what a person from the other team suggests using whatever

body part is suggested (e.g. using mouth, left hand, foot, etc.).

Playing the game: When all members of the team have had a turn, the images are put up and the team talks about how it felt. Each team member is then invited to say something positive about the other team's images.

Note: The chosen subject matter is kept simple (e.g. a house, person, tree).

Variation: Teams are formed and scoring for effort could be made.

Let Rorschach Help Your Story

Objective:	To help develop creative awareness and to explore what exactly is going on in life and look at possible solutions. It is particularly good for working on confidence issues.
Age range:	5+
Group size:	2 to 10
Materials:	Very large sheet of paper, ready mixed paint, pen and A4 (Letter) paper
Creating time:	15 minutes
Playing time:	25 minutes
Creating the game:	In two groups get each group to pour a little paint onto the centre of the large sheet of paper. Tell them they have to jointly make decisions about colours, making sure that not

too much paint is poured. Next, ensure the paper is folded into half and the paint spread with hands. Then get them to open up the paper.

Playing the game: Each person is invited to brainstorm the image and make a piece of creative writing (e.g. a poem or story using the brainstormed words). A time limit is set. The game element is that the most creative piece of writing wins. Here everyone can be a judge.

The group is invited to talk about how it felt to take part in this project

Future City

Objective:	To develop independence through raising awareness and practising negotiating skills.
Age range:	10+
Group size:	2 to 5
Materials:	A very large sheet of paper, several sheets of white A4 (Letter) paper, coloured marker pens, crayons, paints, paint brushes, white glue (PVA)
Creating time:	At least 30 minutes, but activity can go on for more than one session.
Playing time:	At least 30 minutes.
Creating the game:	Explain the aims and rules of the game. Tell them that this game enables young people to

bring to the fore what they feel is important to them.

1. Select a town planner from the group. Instruct this young person to get ideas for their town from the rest of the group and write down or draw all suggestions on a whiteboard or flip chart.

2. Give the rest of the group different responsibilities in the forming of the town – e.g. people in charge of parks, public buildings, sports facilities and public and private transport.

3. Get the young people to make all the decisions. If there are omissions, this is OK as it is their own town.

Playing the game: Once the town is formed the children/young people should have lots of time to play with it – including using other objects such as toy cars and people. This is an excellent game for imaginative play.

Variations: Other themes can be used, e.g. hospital, supermarket, seascape, wildlife forest, etc.

Happy Families

Objective:	To build confidence through sharing and exploring family issues, examining what exactly a family is in this day of diverse family relationships.
Age range:	7+
Group size:	2 to 10
Materials:	Six small white cards for each participant, coloured marker pens, pencils, rulers, scissors
Creating time:	At least 40 minutes, but activity can go on for more than one session.
Playing time:	At least 20 minutes.
Creating the game:	Explain the aims and rules of the game. Discuss with the group what they think constitutes a family. Get them to think of

alternative family groups and how this will be reflected when they make their card family. Have them portray their family on the cards, one card for each family member. Invite each group member to discuss their choice of family.

Playing the game: These cards come together to make a pack, which is dealt out. Each player will ask a specific person if they have a particular member of the family they are collecting. If the other person does have the card, they have to pass it to the first player, who can then ask again. The first one to collect a whole family is the winner.

Variations: A family group could be animals, trees, etc.

Why Am I Feeling This Way?

Objective:	To help children understand strong feelings and manage them by getting in touch with their emotions and working towards solutions.
Age range:	10+
Group size:	2 to 5
Materials:	A4 (Letter) paper, coloured marker pens, scissors and shoe box, Emotion Sheets
Creating time:	Up to 40 minutes
Playing time:	Up to 20 minutes
Creating the game:	Explain the aims and rules of the game. Focus on the 'Emotion Sheets' (see pp.133–139) to help children identify strong feelings they would like to explore. Get each child to write

down/draw two different problems which may be worrying them. Fold up the bits of paper and put them into a box.

Playing the game: One at a time, each child takes out a problem, which they read to the group. Everyone attempts to produce a solution.

Variation: In pairs, work out a role-play that encompasses both problem and solution.

Large Group Scribble

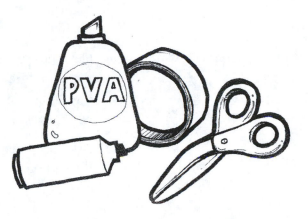

Objectives:	To enable children to be confident in feeling free to tap into their imagination and to know that they are in control of themselves.
Age range:	5+
Group size:	5 to 10
Materials:	Very large white paper, coloured marker pens, oil pastels, white glue (PVA), clear sticky tape, scissors, masking tape
Creating time:	15 minutes
Playing time:	1 hour 15 minutes
Creating the game:	Fix the paper onto the table, so it doesn't move, and have drawing materials close by. Be the time keeper. Invite the group to arm themselves with drawing materials.

Playing the game:

1. Get the group to scribble for five minutes on signal.

2. Stop them, put drawing materials aside and now invite them to walk into the scribble in their minds and say where they are and how it feels.

3. After each person has had a turn invite them to tear the image into small pieces for five minutes.

4. Get the group to gather up as many pieces as they can and make the pieces into something (e.g. a collage, jewellery, a mask, etc.).

5. Ask for feedback about how it felt throughout the exercise, starting with the scribble.

Against Time

Objective:	To build up confidence and independence by allowing children to make decisions for themselves.
Age range:	7+
Group size:	2 to 10
Materials:	Large paper, coloured marker pens, coloured pencils, sand timer
Creating time:	5 minutes
Playing time:	Up to 35 minutes
Creating the game:	Explain the rules of the game. Instruct one child to draw an object, e.g. a tree, a TV or objects from other cultures/countries (if necessary help here with images).

Playing the game:　　A timer is set; the first person to guess which physical or cultural setting the drawing belongs to becomes the next one to draw. Teams and scoring can be made prior to the start of the game.

Alphabet with Feeling

Objective:	To raise self-esteem through acknowledging positive attributes.
Age range:	7+
Group size:	5 to 10
Materials:	Cards, coloured marker pens, ruler, scissors, set of alphabet cards
Creating time:	5 minutes
Playing time:	25 minutes
Creating the game:	Make a set of alphabet cards prior to the session. Explain the aims and rules of the game.
Playing the game:	A circle is formed. The first person picks a card with a letter on it and makes a positive

statement about the person next to them. For example, if an 'A' is picked they could say something like 'I think you are an assertive person' or 'I think you are arty', etc. Then they can go on to the next letter and the next person.

Variation: They could also say a positive statement about themselves before going on to saying something about the next person, with the chosen letter.

Cube Fun

Objectives:	To raise awareness of personal problems and to come up with solutions.
Age range:	7+
Group size:	5 to 10
Materials:	A4 (Letter) thin card, coloured marker pens, glue stick
Creating time:	30 minutes
Playing time:	30 minutes
Creating the game:	Explain the aims and rules of the game. Measure, rule and cut out a cube as shown on the template (p.131). Instruct the participants to write three positive and three not-so-positive things about themselves on the faces of the cube (e.g. talented, clever, intelligent,

friendly, musical; or quick-tempered, impatient, fussy, stubborn) and decorate it with a symbol illustrating the word – a smiley face for friendly, musical notes for musical, for instance. Once this is done form the cube.

Playing the game: Each person throws the cube and reads out the word on the top. The person then elaborates on the word in a positive way, so owning the sentiments.

Variation: Use the word shown on the face to relate a real-life story or incident.

Area Awareness Spinning Top

Objectives:	To enable young people to express how it feels to be in society at this moment in time. To find confidence to cope and find ways of doing so.
Age range:	11+
Group size:	2 to 5
Materials:	Circular card, glue stick, ruler, scissors, coloured marker pens, oil pastels, a dice, coloured counters, dowelling
Creating time:	40 minutes
Playing time:	20 minutes
Creating the game:	Give each person a piece of circular card about 5 inches (13cm) in diameter. Encourage them to think of designing an ideal place to live

in and the positive things that would make a difference to their lives. Instruct each person to divide the card into four sections and think of four positive changes they would like to make to their immediate environment, e.g. youth club staying open for seven days a week, etc. Once completed make it into a spinning top by piercing the middle and passing through a piece of dowelling to enable it to spin.

Playing the game: Each person takes it in turn to spin their particular top. When it stops at the section it lands on, the young person is then invited to talk about their choices and why they included what they did.

Variation: If the group is larger, it can be divided into two. Each group then makes a large spinning top, jointly contributing to its content.

Pass the Compliment

Objective:	To raise awareness and self-esteem by confronting different aspects of a child's character.
Age range:	7+
Group size:	5 to 10
Materials:	A4 (Letter) white paper, coloured marker pens, box
Creating time:	20 minutes
Playing time:	40 minutes
Creating the game:	Explain the aims and rules of the game. Ask each group member to draw/write down two positive statements about themselves and two things they would like to change about

themselves. Make a box as shown in the 'box' instructions (p.125).

Playing the game: All the statements are placed in a box. One person picks out a statement, reads it out to the group and decides who the statement belongs to. If they get the choice wrong more than twice, they put the statement back into the box.

Variation: Each group member is asked to write down one positive statement about another member of the group.

What Am I Like?

Objective:	To raise self-esteem through the recognition of positive attributes (skills, qualities, values and attitudes) in well-known people.
Age range:	10+
Group size:	3 to 10
Materials:	Coloured marker pens, sticky labels
Creating time:	10 to 15 minutes
Playing time:	20 minutes to 45 minutes
Creating the game:	Explain the aims and rules of the game. Lead a discussion on what positive attributes are. Come up with some examples. Then get the group to identify well-known people who they consider may have these. This could include fantasy and cartoon characters, sports

people or TV personalities. Write the names on labels and add some of the characteristics identified.

Playing the game: Sitting in a circle a label is chosen and stuck onto the forehead of one group member. They then have to ascertain who this person is by asking about their attributes, after establishing whether they are male or female, living or dead, real or fantasy (e.g. Mother Teresa – a religious icon, humble, compassionate, etc.).

Drawing Blindfold

Objective:	To develop social skills by building up trust in each other and acceptance that, whatever the end result is, it is fun and OK.
Age range:	7+
Group size:	5 to 10
Materials:	Large paper, oil pastels or coloured marker pens or pencils, blindfolds
Creating time:	20 minutes
Playing time:	10 minutes
Creating the game:	Explain the aims and rules of the game. Arrange the children into pairs. Blindfold one child and explain that their partner dictates what is to be drawn, without telling them what it is (e.g. draw a straight line, stop, now

go down, stop, go back, stop, go up = a box). It may be a person, animal, house, etc. Before the blindfold comes off, get the child to guess what they have drawn. When the image is complete tell the partners to swap over.

Note: Instructions have to be very clear for this to succeed.

Playing the game: Each child should take no more than five minutes for their turn. When the image is complete the children share (a) how it felt to draw something without being able to see and (b) what they feel about the results. Children can be in two teams and points awarded for clear instructions and accuracy in guessing.

I'm the Greatest

Objective:	To encourage positive thinking about self and others.
Age range:	7+
Group size:	2 to 5
Materials:	Thin card cut into pieces of 3 by 5 inches (8 by 13cm), enough for each player to have ten pieces, coloured marker pens, crayons, paints, paint brushes
Creating time:	25 minutes
Playing time:	35 minutes
Creating the game:	Explain the aims and rules of the game. Make five Positive Self cards (e.g. I love myself, I'm the greatest, I'm good at most things, I'm a happy person) and five Positive to Others

cards (e.g. I like you, you're special, you're smart).

Playing the game: The cards are spread face down. Each player in turn picks a card and says what is on the card, for example 'I'm smart'. If they are able to successfully express the sentiment on the card, for instance talk successfully about why they think they're smart, they can keep the card. The first player to collect three Positive Self cards and three Positive to Others cards is the winner.

Part III
Creating Games for Raising Self-Awareness

Opposites Attract

Objective:	To raise awareness of different emotions by making five positive cards and five negative cards about themselves using single words such as 'happy' or 'sad'
Age range:	5 +
Group size:	2 to 4
Materials:	Card, coloured marker pens, scissors
Creating time:	20 minutes
Playing time:	20 minutes
Creating the game:	Explain the aims and rules of the game. Get the group to think about the meaning of opposites (e.g. kind/unkind, happy/sad and frustrated/calm). What contributes to these extremes of emotions? Then tell one half

of the group to write the words selected on card (one word to each card) and the other half to draw the emotion, either making an abstract drawing (e.g. red for anger) or a face depicting the emotion.

Playing the game: All the cards are spread face down and each player is invited to pick two cards. If they successfully select two opposite cards, they can keep these if they are able to give an illustration of the words on the cards (e.g. *happy* – 'I'm happy when someone praises me'; *sad* – 'I'm sad when I'm told off').

Variation: The same emotions could be paired together (e.g. angry face with the word *angry*).

Going with Change

Objective:	To learn to cope with change when things don't go as planned.
Age range:	7+
Group size:	2 to 6
Materials:	Whiteboard and pens, large sheet of paper, coloured marker pens
Creating time:	40 minutes
Playing time:	20 minutes
Creating the game:	Explain the aims and rules of the game. Talk about how when unexpected things happen it can be OK and may even be for the best or turn out unexpectedly well. Have a warm-up. On the whiteboard get one child to start a drawing and another to 'accidentally'

jog their arm. Then invite the first child to incorporate the new mark into the drawing, as if it were meant to be there in the first place.

Playing the game: Get children into twos to play this game by doing a drawing and inviting them to jog each other's arms. Keep an eye on this as children can get carried away and chaos may reign. After the images are complete, feed back how the activity went and how it felt to have the image supposedly 'ruined'. Discuss how it was for each child – was it positive or not?

My Patch

Objective:	To raise awareness of territories, personal and others, and dangers that exist, looking at possible solutions.
Age range:	13+
Group size:	2 to 10
Materials:	Large card, glue stick, scissors, coloured marker pens, oil pastels, a dice, coloured counters
Creating time:	1 hour 30 minutes
Playing time:	30 minutes or more
Creating the game:	Explain that this is a large board game made by the group and that it defines the areas in which the young people live and what they mean to them. Start the session with a

discussion about territories, particularly their personal territories and how meaningful they are to the young people. Invite them to talk about their own personal stories and views on this subject. This discussion could happen whilst they are creating the game. As in standard board games, section the board off into territories identified by colour. Have coloured counters for each person – these could be made using card by cutting small circles and colouring each one according to the person's territory. If the person whose colour is, say, red lands on a yellow square, there should be a challenge they have to solve in order to move forward. If they are unsuccessful, they have to move backwards. The young people are experts on this and will undoubtedly come up with appropriate challenges. There could be a 'communal' area in the centre which anybody can go into without being challenged.

Playing the game: The game is played, as with most board games, by starting on the start square and rolling a dice. Each person moves their own counter when it's their turn. The person who reaches the finishing square first wins. The facilitator then leads a discussion of how it felt to make the game and then to play it.

Treasure Hunt

Objective:	To find out from children what they consider to be their strengths and qualities.
Age range:	7+
Group size:	2 to 10
Materials:	4-inch (10cm) squares of white card, coloured marker pens
Creating time:	10 minutes
Playing time:	20 minutes
Creating the game:	Explain the aims and rules of the game. Talk about what 'treasure' is in a general sense. It could be material acquisitions, or health-related. Invite the children to write their talents, skills, qualities and strengths on

cards. Instruct them to put one treasure on each card with their name on the back.

Playing the game: Divide the group into two. Then invite one group to hide their treasures around the room (whilst the other group is not in the room of course). Suggest that the hiding place shouldn't be too remote. Then invite the treasure seekers to find as many treasures as possible. At the end check how many treasures have been found, making sure there is a time limit for finding the treasure. Then reverse the roles. Have the children collect their own treasure cards to take home.

Changing Faces

Objectives:	To learn to cope with change and to raise awareness.
Age range:	7+
Group size:	2 to 10
Materials:	A4 (Letter) paper, coloured marker pens or coloured pencils, sand timer
Creating time:	10 minutes
Playing time:	20 minutes
Creating the game:	Explain the aims and rules of the game. Instruct each child to draw a large face (use the face template on p.127) no smaller than the size of an A4 (Letter) sheet, adding in the basic features.

Playing the game: In pairs each child swaps with their partner who makes a change to the image. Repeat this three times. Then each child is invited to talk about the resulting faces.

Variation: The children can decide the character of the person created, their likes/dislikes, etc.

Shape Town/Village

Objective:	To raise awareness of identity and group dynamics.
Age range:	7+
Group size:	3 to 5 (each group could have a separate shape, e.g. circle, square, triangle)
Materials:	Very large pieces of paper (could be joined together), coloured marker pens, coloured pencils, paint
Creating time:	30 minutes
Playing time:	30 minutes
Creating the game:	Explain the aims and rules of the game. Outline that the idea is to form a town in which absolutely everything is in the designated shape (e.g. circle – the buildings,

people, cars and animals should all be circular in appearance). Once the groups are decided, enable a discussion about what sort of shape the town could be. Make sure each child works on different parts of the town. A 3D effect could be aimed for; in this case it is possible to make houses, etc. out of boxes.

Playing the game: Once a decision about shape has been made, the facilitator will give all the groups a time limit to create their individual town. When the time is up, each group will feed back on how easy or difficult it was to meet the criteria and whether they had in fact met them successfully.

Variation: For the competitive element a large group could be divided into smaller groups, with the first group to complete being the winners.

Where Do I Belong?

Objective:	To develop an awareness of identity and sense of belonging by developing listening skills and confidence.
Age range:	7+
Group size:	3 to 5
Materials:	Sheets of A4 (Letter) white paper, coloured marker pens, coloured pencils
Creating time:	5 minutes
Playing time:	25 minutes
Creating the game:	Prior to the session make a set of cards depicting different types of home or dwelling. Explain the aims and rules of the game. Divide the children into two groups

of five – Teams A and B. Provide each child with paper and something to draw with.

Playing the game: The teacher/facilitator shows the dwelling to the groups and the children have to draw who lives in the dwelling (e.g. nest = bird, igloo = Eskimo). The competitive element is in the speediness of the responses, and a scoring system could be developed and run by the children.

Variation: Get the children to take turns in the teacher's role, which they should be eager to do.

Please Don't Distract Me

Objectives:	To understand just how difficult it can sometimes be to stay focused and to find ways to help with this.
Age range:	7+
Group size:	2 to 10
Materials:	Paper, coloured marker pens, pencils
Creating time:	5 minutes
Playing time:	25 minutes
Creating the game:	Set down the ground rules, which are that no aggression should take place and that, although each person is invited to distract the person drawing, this should be done in a sensitive and orderly way. Ground rules

are important as young people may get a bit overexcited when playing this game.

Playing the game: Person 1 starts drawing a picture of their choice; whilst this is happening Person 2 thinks of ways of distracting Person 1 (e.g. by talking, singing or even dancing). The criterion here is that no actual touching is allowed. As soon as Person 1 is distracted the game stops. Then they swap over. The facilitator should be the timekeeper to measure who can last the longest.

The facilitator should lead a discussion ensuing from the game about how it felt to be distracted, how easy/difficult it was to be the distractee, ways of staying focused, and what other ideas the group may have for a similar or different game to help with the problem of 'staying focused'.

Building Up Clusters

Objective:	To raise self-awareness through exploring feeling words to broaden vocabulary and outlook.
Age range:	10+
Group size:	2 to 10
Materials:	Thesaurus/dictionary, card, coloured marker pens, pencils, rulers, scissors
Creating time:	30 minutes
Playing time:	30 minutes
Creating the game:	Explain the aims and rules of the game. Encourage the group to discuss feeling words (e.g. rage, anger, love, etc.). Then choose one word to focus on and expand it into a cluster (e.g. love – like, fondness, affection, devotion).

Make up cards with the words identified on them, a card for each word. Each person can be responsible for a cluster – although the group would have contributed to it. Use different coloured card for each cluster.

Playing the game: Each person in the group chooses a cluster and makes up a sentence about a person they know relating to their particular cluster. They then share this with the group. They can go on to swap clusters and use the same procedure.

Variation: Clusters could be made of family, friendships, social groups. The group should think of the number of groups they belong to and make clusters.

Changing Circles

Objectives:	To raise awareness of problems and to come up with solutions; to enable each child to externalise their concerns and realise that their problem is also shared by others.
Age range:	10+
Group size:	3 to 10
Materials:	Paper, coloured marker pens, a box (see box instructions on p.125)
Creating time:	20 minutes
Playing time:	20 minutes
Creating the game:	Arrange the room so that the children can sit comfortably in a circle. Explain the aims and rules of the game. First clarify and lead a discussion on the types of problems and

concerns faced by young people (e.g. anger, housing, sibling rivalry, abuse). Explain that the game offers opportunities for the group to find solutions for each other. Sit the group in a circle. Have each child write or draw their problems/concerns, each one on a separate piece of paper, which are then placed face down in a container.

Playing the game: The children take it in turns to choose a problem and think about solutions. The group can then extend this with other solutions. This is done until all the problems have been covered. (Note: The problems are anonymous.)

Scribble Exchange

Objective:	To highlight current issues, enabling the exploration of possible solutions.
Age range:	7+
Group size:	2 to 6
Materials:	Four pieces of A4 (Letter) paper for each participant, coloured marker pens or crayons
Creating time:	10 minutes
Playing time:	30 minutes
Creating the game:	Pair the group up. Then give each person four sheets of paper and some drawing equipment.
Playing the game:	To play the game each person scribbles for three seconds and exchanges the scribble with their partner. Then the partner stares

at the scribble and makes it into something, giving the scribble a name. This process is repeated twice more; with the fourth piece of paper everyone gives themselves a scribble and makes it into something. Each person shares their images and relates how they impact on their lives at this moment in time.

How Do I Feel?

Objective:	To raise self-awareness about different feelings.
Age range:	7+
Group size:	2 to 10
Materials:	Card, coloured marker pens, scissors, score sheet, Emotion Sheet (for examples see pp.133–139)
Creating time:	40 minutes
Playing time:	20 minutes
Creating the game:	Explain the aims and rules of the game. Discuss with the children what emotions are and invite one or two to illustrate what they feel is an emotion. Divide the A4 sheet of card into eight cards. On each card get them

to draw a face with a different emotion and write the word under the drawing. Instruct each child to write their name on the back of each card and decorate.

Playing the game: The game can be played in pairs or groups. First, the cards are spread out face down in front of them. One child picks a card and mimes the emotion on the card and their partner/group has to guess what the emotion is. A correct answer scores a point. When all the cards have been played the person who has the most points wins. A scoring sheet is used for this purpose.

Paper Roll Game

Objective:	To raise awareness about identity issues and the choices that can be made.
Age range:	7+
Group size:	2 to 10
Materials:	A roll of kitchen paper, coloured marker pens
Creating time:	15 minutes
Playing time:	15 minutes
Creating the game:	Instruct each person to take several pieces off the roll. Then invite them to draw something about themselves, one on each sheet (e.g. 'I'm confident' on one sheet and 'I'm shy' on another, etc.).

Playing the game: Each person in turn selects a piece and shares it with the group, citing a particular incident/ story to illustrate the characteristic identified. The group can help with solutions if they are needed (e.g. in 'I'm shy' the group can come up with ideas of what the young person can do to help with this).

The group are invited to talk about how it felt to take part in this project.

Jigsaw – Self-Portrait

Objectives:	To look at identity and raise self-awareness and social skills; to develop dexterity.
Age range:	7+
Group size:	2 to 6
Materials:	A piece of A4 (Letter) card; coloured marker pens, oil pastels or pencils; scissors; timer; shallow box or tray for each team
Creating time:	25 minutes
Playing time:	5 minutes
Creating the game:	Explain the aims and rules of the game. Filling the whole sheet of paper, get each child to draw a self-portrait which is then coloured in (use the face template as a starting point; see p.127). Tell the children to cut their portrait

into pieces. Arrange the group into two teams and then instruct them to place each team's pieces in a large shallow tray or box (one for each team). Use a timer to energise the game. (Note: Use fewer pieces for the younger age group and more for the older.)

Playing the game: The first team to complete all their portraits wins. Here they can learn that by helping each other they can complete the game speedily.

A points system could be worked out (e.g. points gained in the negotiating process, helping each other and finishing). A discussion can be led as to how the game felt, especially cutting up the portrait.

My Patch Spinning Top

Objective:	To enable young people to express how it feels to live in their particular area.
Age range:	13+
Group size:	2 to 6
Materials:	Large piece of card, ruler, large coloured marker pens, scissors, dowelling
Creating time:	20 minutes
Playing time:	40 minutes
Creating the game:	Instruct the group to make a 12-inch (30cm) circular spinning top. Cut a circle from the card and through discussion divide the card into sections of their postcodes (e.g. E8, E5, N16, etc.) or home areas. Make up the top by

piercing a hole in the centre and passing a piece of dowelling into it.

Playing the game: Each person takes it in turn to spin the top. According to which section it lands on, the young person is then invited to talk about this – why they included it and any incidents/stories they would like to share with the group. A discussion is led about how to cope when incidents occur. The facilitator could encourage the group to look at other boroughs and big cities too.

Playing Detective

Objective:	To raise awareness through problem solving.
Age range:	10+
Group size:	2 to 5
Materials:	Five small white cards for each participant, coloured marker pens, coloured pencils
Creating time:	30 minutes
Playing time:	30 minutes
Creating the game:	Explain the aims and rules of the game. Invite discussion as to what a crime could be – its wide spectrum. Get the children to say what a crime is for them personally (e.g. bullying, abuse, drug taking, etc.). Get them to make five crime cards each using drawings and words.

Playing the game: All the cards are placed face down. One person at a time draws a card. They can then relate a real-life incident/story, which may not necessarily involve them. This is where the detective work begins. The group should identify whose card this may be and finally how this crime could be solved. There shouldn't be any judgement made towards any group member, rather praise for having the courage to talk about issues.

Listening and Responding

Objective:	To enhance children's listening skills and spatial awareness using the left hand if right-handed and vice versa.
Age range:	7+
Group size:	2 to 10
Materials:	White paper, coloured marker pens, coloured pencils
Creating time:	50 minutes (for a large group)
Playing time:	30 minutes
Creating the game:	If the group is large, divide it into two teams. Get one child from each team to draw. Instruct them to use their non-drawing hand and have them follow your drawing instructions (e.g. draw a bird in a tree).

Playing the game: Continue the game with the rest of the children and have a time limit of five minutes for each drawing. Award points for the best drawings. Let the groups help with recording the points awarded. Repeat the process until each person has had a turn.

Ask the children for their responses to the game and invite any suggestions they may have.

Please Pass the…

Objective:	To learn social interaction, co-operation and patience through getting children negotiating with each other and realising that sensitivity gets them a long way.
Age range:	7+
Group size:	4 to 6
Materials:	A4 (Letter) paper or larger; coloured marker pens, coloured pencils and oil pastels; large room/hall
Creating time:	20 minutes
Playing time:	30 minutes
Creating the game:	Explain the aims and rules of the game. Arrange the materials in separate areas which are sectioned out using masking tape or four

PE mats – paper in one area, pens in another, etc. Put a child in charge of each section. The idea is for each child to collect enough materials to make a drawing of their own.

Playing the game: First each child collects the materials. To do this they will have to negotiate with each other until they have a full set of all materials. They can then commence a drawing of their choice. The first to finish wins.

Variation: A gallery of the pictures could be formed and voting could take place on content, artistic skill, creativity and imagination. Scoring could be introduced for this.

Who Am I?

Objective:	To develop an awareness of feelings and body awareness.
Age range:	7 to 11
Group size:	2 to 10
Materials:	Sheets of A4 (Letter) white paper decorated with a grid, coloured marker pens, coloured pencils
Creating time:	5 minutes
Playing time:	25 minutes
Creating the game:	Explain the aims and rules of the game. Divide the children into two groups. Give each child some paper and something to draw with.

Playing the game: The teacher has a list of simple objects, and describes each object by giving them a clue. The children have to say what they think the object is – e.g. 'Something you sleep on' (answer: 'Bed') or 'Something with four legs you can eat on', (answer: 'Table').

When they have grasped how to play, they draw their answers, but do not call out, to words relating to 'Who am I?' – e.g. 'Something you use to think with', (answer: 'Brain') or 'Something you use to feel with' (answer: 'Heart'). The facilitator makes it progressively harder depending on how they get on. A point for each correct answer may be given and the team with the most correct answers wins.

Variation: This game may be used on a one-to-one basis to encourage a child to talk about feelings and where they can be felt (e.g. in which part of your body would you feel a headache, anger, sadness, etc.).

Useful Templates and Resources

Box

Fold a piece of A4 thin card in half and half again in the landscape position, then unfold. Now fold the card in half and half again in the portrait position. Make sure each time you make a fold to crease it down firmly. When you unfold you should end up with a piece of card with a grid as shown in the diagram.

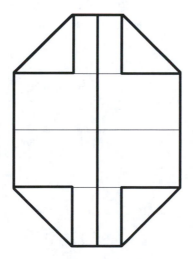

In the landscape position now fold the sides to the middle. Then fold the corners to the nearest horizontal crease.

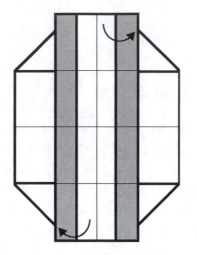

Where the edges of the paper meet in the centre, fold back along the vertical side of the corner flap, to finish as shown in the diagram.

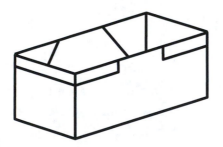

Take hold of the centre of each of the vertical flaps you have just created and pull outwards to form a box shape. Pinch the sides to straighten.

Face

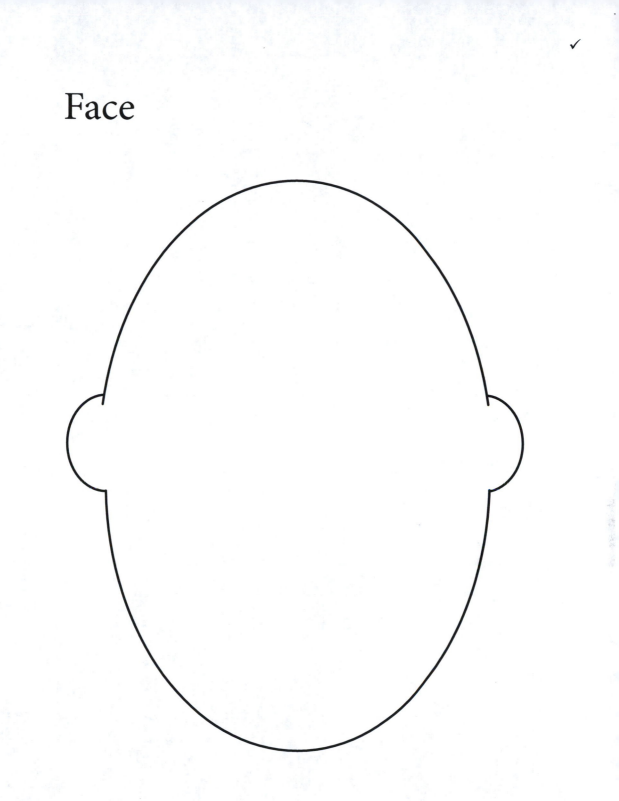

Rabbit's Ears

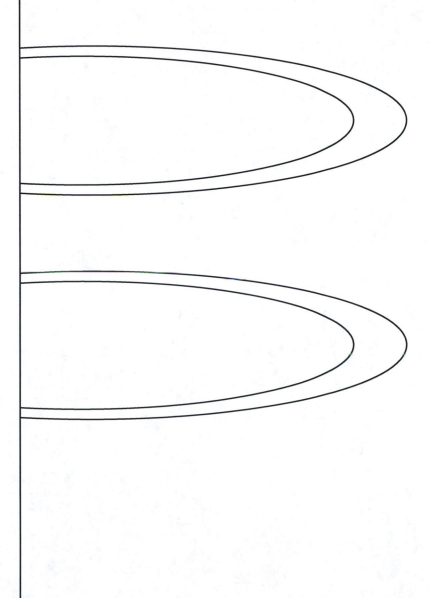

Cube

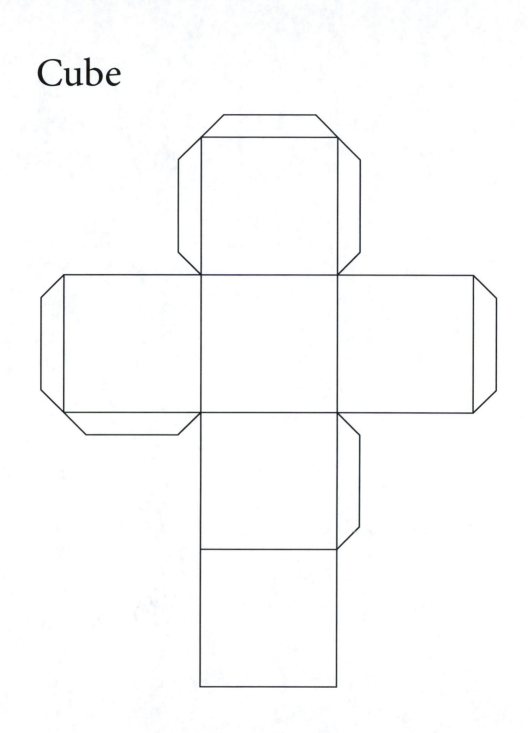

Emotion Sheet 1

Emotion Sheet 2

Emotion Sheet 3

Emotion Sheet 4

Creative Coping Skills for Children

Emotional Support through Arts and Crafts Activities

Bonnie Thomas

ISBN 9781843109211
Paperback: £18.99/$29.95

Everyone has different needs when it comes to coping with life's stressors, and children are no different. Some need quiet and soothing activities to calm them down, whereas others require more physical activity or intense sensory input to relax their minds and bodies.

This resource comprises a collection of fun, flexible, tried-and-tested activities, and make-it-yourself workbooks for parents and professionals to help a child in need of extra emotional support find the coping skills that fit them best. Each activity lists the materials required and includes clear directions for how to do it. There is something for every child: whether they are dynamic and creative or more cerebral and literal. Projects include making wish fairies, dream catchers, and mandalas; managing unstructured time with activities such as creating comics, dioramas, and tongue twisters; and simple ideas for instant soothing, such as taking deep breaths, blowing bubbles, making silly faces, and playing music. *Creative Coping Skills for Children* also includes specific interventions for anxious or grieving children such as making worry dolls and memory shrines.

This book is full of fun, easy, creative project ideas for parents of children aged 3–12, teachers, counselors, play therapists, social workers, and all professionals working with children.

Bonnie Thomas LCSW is a school-based clinician, providing individual and family therapy to children aged 3–12. She has also worked in the Juvenile Corrections System and coordinated a mentoring programme for young girls living in public housing.

Arts Activities for Children and Young People in Need

Helping Children to Develop Mindfulness, Spiritual Awareness and Self-Esteem

Diana Coholic

ISBN 9781849050012
Paperback: £19.99/$32.95

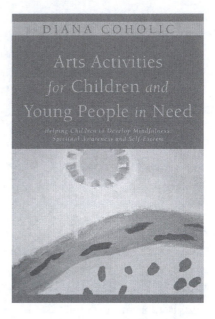

Art-based activities can develop resilience and self-esteem, enabling children in need to cope better with ongoing stress and loss. *Arts Activities for Children and Young People in Need* offers interventions and exercises drawn from practice and research, for practitioners to use as a basis for their own arts-based groups or one-to-one sessions.

Holistic arts activities facilitate a spiritually sensitive approach. Mindfulness-based exercises underpin the approach, and include guided meditations in which a group imagines that they are clouds, or draw feelings and emotions while listening to music, to encourage awareness of the senses. The activities help the group to relax and become more self-aware, encourage an exploration of feelings, values and understanding and are beneficial for children not ready to embrace traditional therapies or counselling.

This book is accessible and suitable for helping, health and education practitioners and students from a variety of disciplines, such as social work, psychology and counselling.

Diana Coholic is Associate Professor in the School of Social Work at Laurentian University, Canada. Her research programme studies the effectiveness of holistic arts-based methods with children who have significant problems. She has been a social work practitioner for 18 years, and also maintains a small private practice working with children and young people.

Self-Esteem Games for Children

Deborah M. Plummer

Illustrated by Jane Serrurier

ISBN 9781843104247
Paperback: £14.99/$29.95

'This is a clearly written, logically organised, practical handbook. Excellent. Thoroughly recommended.'

–Play for Life (Play Therapy)

In this practical handbook, self-esteem expert Deborah Plummer offers a wealth of familiar and easy-to-learn games carefully chosen to build and maintain self-esteem in children aged 5–11.

The selection of games reflects the seven key elements of healthy self-esteem – self-knowledge, self and others, self-acceptance, self-reliance, self-expression, self-confidence and self-awareness – and includes opportunities for thinking and discussion. The book combines physically active and passive games, verbal and non-verbal games and games for pairs or groups, which makes them equally accessible for children with speech/language difficulties or those with physical disabilities. Deborah Plummer shows that the games can be easily adapted and she encourages readers to be creative in inventing their own alternative versions.

This is an ideal resource for teachers, parents, carers and all those working to nurture self-esteem in children.

Deborah M. Plummer is a registered speech and language therapist and imagework practitioner with over 20 years' experience of facilitating groups and working individually with both children and adults. Formerly a clinical lead therapist working within the NHS, she is now a clinical supervisor and lecturer and runs workshops and short courses on the uses of imagery and issues of self-esteem in the UK and abroad. She is the author of *Helping Children to Build Self-Esteem* (2nd edition), *Helping Adolescents and Adults to Build Self-Esteem*, *The Adventures of the Little Tin Tortoise: A Self-esteem Story* and *Using Interactive Imagework with Children*, all published by Jessica Kingsley Publishers.